P9-BZR-562

BRUSH THEIR TEETH

by Thomas Kingsley Troupe

illustrated by Jamey Christoph

PICTURE WINDOW BOOKS
a capstone imprint

Kitanai the Origami Dog loved to jump and play around the pond. One day he leapt from lily pad to lily pad. He didn't want to fall into the water.

As he jumped across the pond,
a crocodile rose to the surface.

Ow, my choppers!
What's the matter, big guy?
Some of my teeth really hurt. Maybe that's why they call me Cavity Croc.

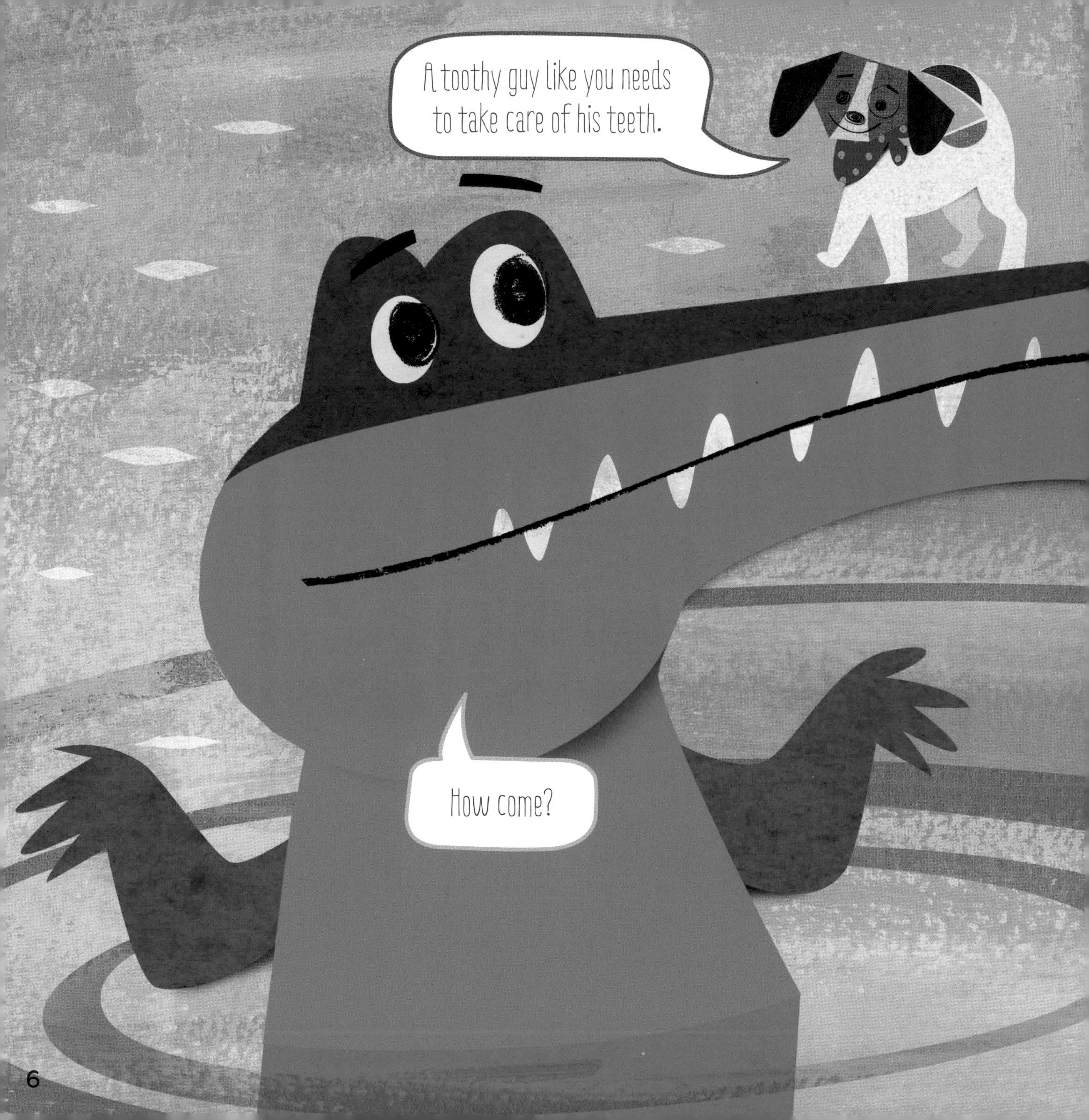
A toothy guy like you needs to take care of his teeth.
How come?

Healthy teeth help you chew and talk. They also make you look nice when you smile.
Do you like soup?
Sometimes.
Well, if all your teeth fall out, that might be all you can eat!

8

9

13

Wow! Brushing my teeth made a big difference. My teeth don't feel so fuzzy!

15

You should also floss daily!
Is floss like string?
Sort of, but floss is waxy so it can slide between your teeth. Flossing frees up any food stuck in there.
Dental
FLOSS

17

To make sure your teeth look and stay healthy, you should visit a dentist.

The dentist will check and clean your teeth and gums. The best part? You'll get a new toothbrush!

18

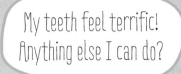

GLOSSARY

acid—a strong liquid that can break down teeth

bacteria—very small living things that exist all around you and inside you; some bacteria cause disease

decay—to break down or rot

gum—the firm flesh found at the base of a tooth

plaque—the coating of food, spit, and bacteria that forms on teeth and can cause them to break down

READ MORE

Huelin, Jodi. *A Cavity Is a Hole in Your Tooth.* Collins, N.Y.: Harper, 2010.

Rissman, Rebecca. *Should Billy Brush His Teeth: Taking Care of Yourself.* Chicago: Heinemann Library, 2013.

Tourville, Amanda Doering. *Brush, Floss, Rinse: Caring For Your Teeth and Gums.* Minneapolis: Picture Window Books, 2009.

INTERNET SITES

FactHound offers a safe, fun way to find Internet sites related to this book. All of the sites on FactHound have been researched by our staff.

Here's all you do:

Visit *www.facthound.com*

Type in this code: 9781479560806

Check out projects, games and lots more at
www.capstonekids.com

INDEX

Editor: Jeni Wittrock
Designer: Ashlee Suker
Art Director: Nathan Gassman
Production Specialist: Laura Manthe
The illustrations in this book were created digitally.

Picture Window Books are published by Capstone,
1710 Roe Crest Drive, North Mankato, Minnesota 56003
www.capstonepub.com

Copyright © 2015 by Picture Window Books, a Capstone imprint.
All rights reserved. No part of this publication may be reproduced in whole
or in part, or stored in a retrieval system, or transmitted in any form or by
any means, electronic, mechanical, photocopying, recording, or otherwise,
without written permission of the publisher.

Library of Congress Cataloging-in-Publication
Troupe, Thomas Kingsley.
Kitanai and Cavity Croc brush their teeth/by Thomas
Kingsley Troupe.
pages cm.—(Nonfiction Picture Books. Kitanai's Healthy Habits)
Summary: "Kitanai the dog teaches Cavity Croc how to keep teeth
clean"—Provided by publisher.
Audience: Ages 5–7
Audience: K to grade 3
ISBN 978-1-4795-6116-2 (eBook pdf)
ISBN 978-1-4795-6080-6 (library binding)
ISBN 978-1-4795-6112-4 (paperback)
1. Teeth—Care and hygiene—Juvenile literature. I. Title.
RK63.T76 2015
617.60083—dc23
2014021102

Printed in the United States of America in North Mankato, Minnesota
102014   008482CGS15

Other titles in this series:

Kitanai and Filthy Flamingo
WASH UP
by Thomas Kingsley Troupe
Illustrated by Jenny Christoph

Kitanai and Hungry Hare
EAT HEALTHFULLY
by Thomas Kingsley Troupe
Illustrated by Jenny Christoph

Kitanai and Lazy Lizard
GET FIT
by Thomas Kingsley Troupe
Illustrated by Jenny Christoph